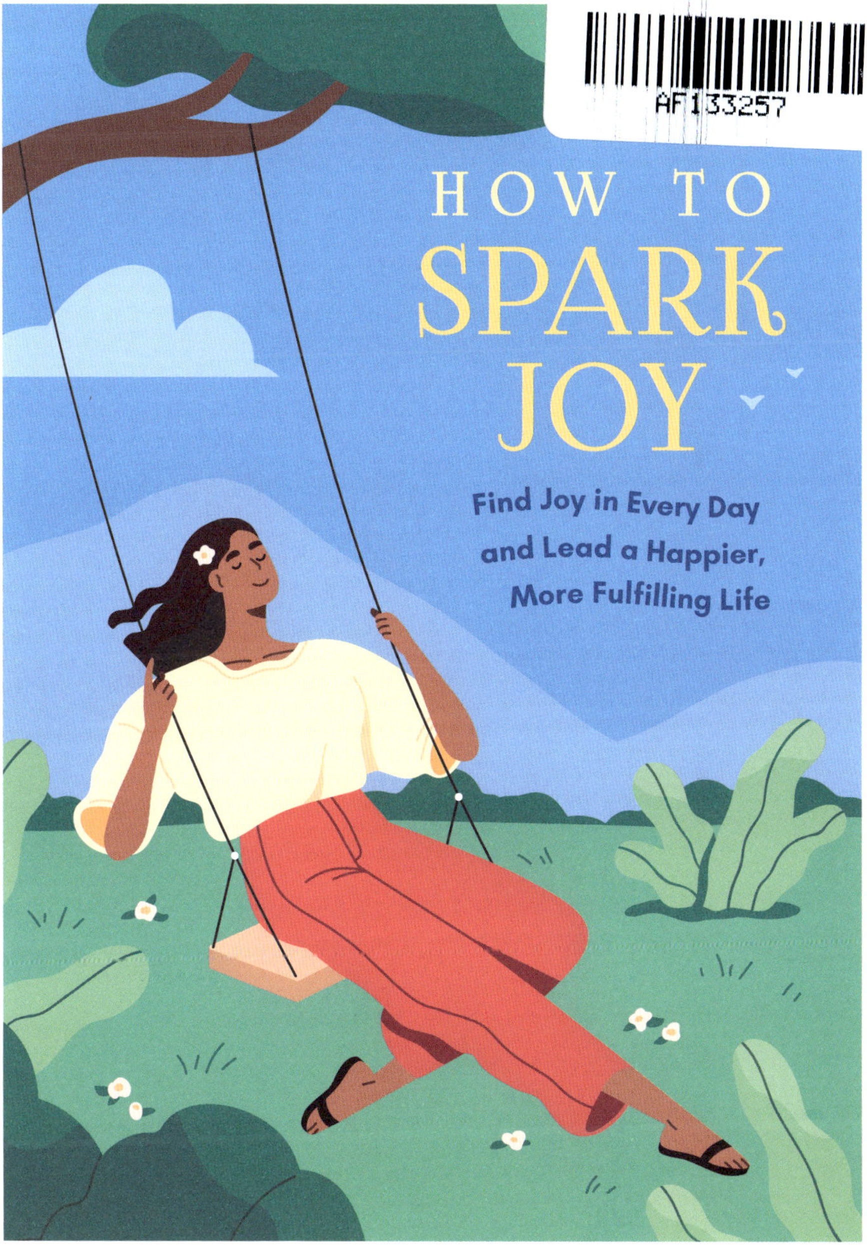

HOW TO SPARK JOY

Find Joy in Every Day and Lead a Happier, More Fulfilling Life

Sophie Golding

vie

HOW TO SPARK JOY

Copyright © Octopus Publishing Group Limited, 2026

All rights reserved.

Text by Caroline Roope

No part of this book may be reproduced by any means, nor transmitted, nor translated into a machine language, without the written permission of the publishers.

Condition of Sale
This book is sold subject to the condition that it shall not, by way of trade or otherwise, be lent, resold, hired out or otherwise circulated in any form of binding or cover other than that in which it is published and without a similar condition including this condition being imposed on the subsequent purchaser.

An Hachette UK Company
www.hachette.co.uk

Vie Books, an imprint of Summersdale Publishers
Part of Octopus Publishing Group Limited
Carmelite House
50 Victoria Embankment
LONDON
EC4Y 0DZ
UK

This FSC® label means that materials and other controlled sources used for the product have been responsibly sourced

www.summersdale.com

The authorized representative in the EEA is Hachette Ireland, 8 Castlecourt Centre, Dublin 15, D15 XTP3, Ireland (email: info@hbgi.ie)

Printed and bound in China

ISBN: 978-1-83799-749-7
eISBN: 978-1-83799-750-3

Substantial discounts on bulk quantities of Summersdale books are available to corporations, professional associations and other organizations. For details contact general enquiries: telephone: +44 (0) 1243 771107 or email: enquiries@summersdale.com.

CONTENTS

Introduction
5

Chapter One:
What Is "Sparking Joy"?
6

Chapter Two:
Happy Mind
44

Chapter Three:
Happy Body
80

Chapter Four:
Joyful Life
120

Conclusion
157

INTRODUCTION

Welcome to *How to Spark Joy*, an inspiring book of tips, quotes and affirmations to help you find joy in everyday experiences.

Knowing how to spark joy is essential for our well-being. In a world where stress, responsibilities and demands on our time are frequently the norm, nurturing joyful moments might feel like an impossible task. And when we do manage to create them, we're often too preoccupied with the mundanity of life to really appreciate the experience. But by picking up this book, you're already setting an intention to go on a joyful journey and bring light into your life – go you!

In this book, we'll look at what "sparking joy" means, plus how a happy mindset and positive self-image are key to living a joyful life. Finally, we'll discover how, by prioritizing joy, you'll be giving yourself the best chance of living a happy life.

Ready? Let's go spark some joy!

CHAPTER ONE

WHAT IS "SPARKING JOY"?

Of all the positive emotions we experience as humans, feeling joyful is a choice. It can be nurtured and enjoyed, regardless of our circumstances. While happiness is largely dependent on external factors, joy often comes from within. From inner peace to deep satisfaction, contentment or pure delight – you don't have to wait for your life to change or attain a level of perfection in your existence to cultivate joy. Sparking joy is simply the act of doing more of the things that make you happy, finding balance in your life and nurturing a happy mind and body. Put (very) simply, the more joy you spark, the more joyful your life will be.

Joy is the holy fire that keeps our purpose warm and our intelligence aglow.

Helen Keller

SMALL SPARK, WARM GLOW

It's easy to feel deflated if we think our lives don't measure up in some way. Whether you're trying to live up to someone else's idea of "perfect", or you've set your own impossible expectations of what happy looks like, if you're feeling more joyless than joyful in life, it's probably time to reframe your outlook.

Research has proven that practising joy improves our brainpower and ability to succeed in life. If you've convinced yourself that achieving success will lead to everlasting joyfulness, it's time for a reality check, because the opposite is actually true.

So what's the solution? Instead of focusing on making the rest of your life as perfect as it can be, in the hope that happiness will be the ultimate prize, try thinking about what can bring you joy right now. Micro-moments of bliss can be just as impactful as a big explosion of happiness – and they're easier to attain. Whether it's a steaming mug of hot chocolate on a chilly day or a barefoot walk on damp grass, ultimately it's the little things that build a big, joyful picture – and they cost less, too!

PRESENT PERFECT

Stop for a moment and look around. What do you see? Whether it's the four walls of the room you're sitting in or a vast landscape unfolding before you, at this point in time, none of us is guaranteed anything more than what we have right here in this moment. We're not guaranteed wealth or a bigger home, and we're certainly not guaranteed good health and a long life. The point is that we can't predict the future, so why not focus on finding and creating joy right now? Choosing joy is the easiest (and best) choice you'll make today – and that *is* guaranteed.

I believe a joyful life is made up of joyful moments gracefully strung together.

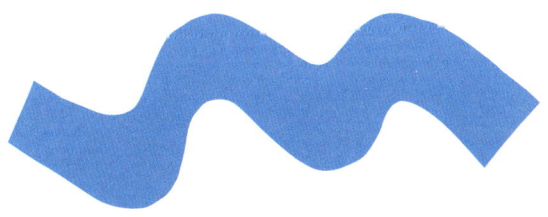

Brené Brown

MAKE A JOY LIST

Being able to list what gives you all the good feels sounds relatively simple, but when was the last time you stopped to think about what really makes you happy? Whether it's spending time with friends or pursuing your passions, sometimes your brain just needs a little nudge in the right direction. When life gets busy, it's easy to forget what joy feels like, but once you've worked out what gives you that warm, fuzzy glow inside, you can start to work out how to make more time for it.

Choose to add joy and fulfilment to your life

PUT JOY ON YOUR AGENDA

In the hustle and bustle of a busy life, finding time to focus on joy often feels a little selfish and overindulgent – after all, it can be difficult to justify sparking joy when you're knee-deep in parenting or you've got a work commitment to fulfil.

But joy isn't something that requires a ton of planning, culminating in a grand moment with a fanfare – it's something that can be found in small, everyday moments. The key is to prioritize it, even if it's just for a few minutes each day. Taking a moment to feel contented isn't selfish – it's self-care, and something we're all deserving of.

Whether it's listening to some calming music for 10 minutes or even just stepping outside to breathe some fresh air, simple acts can offer a sense of fulfilment. The important thing is to be intentional and allow yourself time for these moments. Make space for whatever lights up your joy-o-meter and you'll soon realize it's the small things we do for ourselves that have the biggest impact.

Joy does not simply happen to us. We have to choose joy and keep choosing it every day.

Henri Nouwen

When you wish someone joy, you wish them peace, love, prosperity, happiness... all the good things.

Maya Angelou

JOYFUL YOU

Joy is good for our minds and bodies – a fact that's been proven by research. Studies have shown it reduces stress, cultivates resilience and enhances our well-being. It's also been proven to boost our mood and promote a sense of fulfilment.

Beyond the benefits to ourselves, joy is also contagious – it uplifts and inspires others, creating a ripple effect that can positively influence those around us. In a world that likes to throw curveballs at us every so often, cultivating joy helps maintain balance, offering a reminder that even when things feel tough, there is always space for happiness and light.

Joy is what happens to us when we allow ourselves to recognize how good things really are.

Marianne Williamson

THE JOURNEY TO JOY

To be able to spark joy, you need to work out what joy means to you. Take some time to reflect on the moments in your life that have made you feel most alive and fulfilled. Perhaps your joy comes from quiet solitude, or maybe it's sparked through social connection. It could even be linked to an activity you enjoy or creative expression. Tune in to your emotions, taking time to understand your values and what lights you up. If it's something that resonates with your authentic self and enriches your daily life, you're on the right track.

HAPPILY EVER AFTER...

Humans seem to be programmed with the belief that happiness must be earned. "If I can just get this promotion, *then* I'll be happy." "When I get straight As in my exams, *then* I'll be happier." Sound familiar? That's because many of us feel we don't deserve to be happy. This is, of course, nonsense, but our default setting is to expect happiness to arise from external influences, rather than drawing on our own emotional resources. And because we tend to move the goalposts again once we've attained whatever it is we *think* we need to be happy, we can get stuck in a cycle of dissatisfaction and frustration.

But know this: happiness is already inside each and every one of us. In fact, it's at the core of our existence as humans and is as important as eating, sleeping and breathing. It's vital for our well-being. When we're happy, we're able to connect with others and spark joy in those around us – and our lives take on more meaning and purpose.

Start to accept that you don't need to earn your happiness. Your happiness starts with you – just as you are.

PERMISSION GRANTED

Every day, give yourself permission to do something for no other reason than that it brings you joy. It could be 10 minutes of mindful colouring or having a catch-up (or even a pillow fight!) with your friends. The more fun, the better! Adulting rarely allows you to do something purely for amusement, so challenge yourself to create a bite-sized spark of joy in your day.

START YOUR DAY THE JOYFUL WAY

Starting your day with a positive mindset is a really straightforward way to spark some joy before you face whatever challenges life has in store for you. As we discovered at the beginning of the chapter, it's all about choice. Granted, it's difficult to get excited about your day if you're facing household chores, a tax return or some other mind-numbingly mundane task, but you absolutely *can* decide to embrace positivity and make your day a good one. Marvellous or miserable – only you can decide.

TAKE A MOMENT TO BREATHE

How much attention do you pay to your breathing? You just do it without thinking, right? But if you take a moment to really concentrate on each breath you take, it will bring your focus back to yourself, allowing you a few joyful minutes to just *be*. You could try it right now! Here's how to do it:

1. Stop what you're doing and take a deep breath. Feel your lungs expanding.
2. Hold the breath for a second or two.
3. Calmly let it all out and enjoy the sensation of your chest falling. You could add in a big sigh at the same time, if you feel like it.
4. Now repeat once more.

How was that? Hopefully, that little moment in time allowed you to refocus your attention on yourself, rather than whatever is happening around you. It's also a really helpful technique to use in those moments when you're feeling overwhelmed and not at all joyful, because although when this happens you might feel a long way from being happy, it'll be the first step to regaining a sense of calm and perspective.

Choose joy,
and joy will choose you

You are the key to a life filled with joy

SMILE TO SPARK JOY

Smiling is good for us, according to research published in the journal *Health Psychology Review*. This 2023 study found that each time you smile, the feel-good hormones dopamine, endorphins and serotonin throw a little party in your brain. And guess who's invited? You!

Not only that, but when you smile, you feel more relaxed and your heart rate and blood pressure decrease, alleviating feelings of anxiety and helping boost your mood. Smiling is also contagious, so it's the quickest way to spark joy – not just for you, but for those around you, too.

Keep your face always towards the sunshine, and the shadows will fall behind you.

M. B. Whitman

Don't focus on
the finish line –
find joy in the
journey instead

We do not remember days,
we remember moments.

Cesare Pavese

FIND THE SILVER LINING

When dark clouds gather in our lives, it can be difficult to see the sun trying to shine through. It's at these moments – when we're furthest from experiencing joy – that being able to find the silver lining makes a difference. It's about shifting perspective. Next time you're facing a challenging situation, see it as an opportunity for growth. Find joy in a lesson learned, and marvel at your resilience to square up to adversity and tackle it head-on. While setbacks in life are inevitable, humans have a remarkable ability to make the best of things. You're more resilient than you realize.

BANISH THAT MENTAL BLOCK

Sometimes our brains start to work against us and we get stuck in a cycle of negative thinking that blocks our ability to embrace joy. We start to focus on worries, doubts or past failures, rather than appreciating the present moment. Our minds become clouded by a negative narrative, and we start to believe that life must be "better" or "perfect" before we can truly be happy.

As humans, we're also pretty bad at showing self-compassion. We can be overly critical of ourselves, which diminishes our sense of worth and makes it even harder for us to feel joyful. And that's before we've even considered the influence of external factors, such as work stress, financial anxieties or toxic relationships.

Yet even in these circumstances, joy can still be found if we learn how to shift our focus, practise gratitude and cultivate a positive mindset – all of which we'll be exploring in the following chapters. For many of us, it's our own behaviours and thinking patterns that provide the biggest blockages to joy. By learning how to recognize and reframe the way we think about ourselves and the world around us, we can open our minds and bodies to greater happiness and joy.

Worry never robs tomorrow of its sorrow; it only saps today of its joy.

Leo Buscaglia

START A ROUTINE REBELLION

Who fancies a little anarchy in their life? Breaking free from your daily routine can gift endless amounts of joy. After all, it's exhilarating doing something unplanned and unexpected.

Let's be honest: many of us love a routine and would be lost without some semblance of order in our lives – but where's the joy in that? Surprises of the good variety, such as a friend popping round unexpectedly or a last-minute invite somewhere exciting, are joyful opportunities that it would be a travesty to miss. So before you turn down that hastily organized trip just because you weren't expecting it, consider doing something spontaneous for once, just for fun.

MAKE TIME FOR ALTRUISM

Being altruistic is both selfish and selfless. Yes, really! Helping others not only makes the recipient of our kindness happy, but it also presents an opportunity to make ourselves happy, too. Altruistic acts trigger the release of endorphins and oxytocin, hormones linked to happiness, joy and well-being. They also boost our self-esteem and enable us to make those all-important joy-sparking connections with fellow humans. Demonstrating compassion and a sense of humanity fosters joy in the deepest and truest sense of the word. It'll not only make someone else's day, but it'll make yours, too. What small act of kindness could you perform today?

CHAPTER TWO

HAPPY MIND

Cultivating a happy mindset is crucial for living joyfully. A positive outlook will help you navigate life's challenges with resilience, as well as reframe setbacks as opportunities for learning and growth. Happy-minded people have also been shown to forge stronger relationships with others and feel less stressed and more motivated to achieve their goals.

Nurturing all those good feels takes a little time and effort but can have a profound impact on your overall health and ability to find joy in everyday moments. It's one of the kindest things you can do for yourself – after all, if you look after your mind, it will look after you. Read on to discover how to start your mind on its joyful journey…

Find joy in
the little things

SAY "NO"
TO NEGATIVITY

It's perfectly normal to carry a little negativity around with us every day. It's no easy task feeling joyful 24/7 when the washing machine has flooded the kitchen, there's a power cut and you've got friends coming around for dinner in half an hour. Life can be unpredictable, which can make us anxious, meaning it's easier for negative thoughts to take hold. We can't control everything, but we can choose to challenge our negative thoughts and change our perspectives. Here's a simple way to start right now:

CATCH, CHECK, CHALLENGE AND CHANGE

Catch: Take a tiny moment to catch the thought. For example, "I messed something up. I'm terrible at my job."

Check: Do you have any factual evidence to support the negative thought? For example, "I made a mistake, but I normally perform well."

Challenge: What evidence is there to contradict the thought? For example, "Yesterday my boss noted my team-player ethos and wants me to apply for a promotion."

Change: Can you reframe the thought and make it more balanced? For example, "I'm having a difficult day. It'll be hard to find a solution, but my boss will see I tried my best to rectify the error."

PRIORITIZE AND PROTECT YOUR PEACE

Imagine being able to draw from a well of calmness and contentment whenever life gets a bit too much. Looking after your inner peace means your mind will be more open to joy and the happiness that follows. It's not an escape from reality (although that can seem tempting at times!), but rather a tool you can use to face sticky situations with resilience. If you're not sure where your happy place is, you could try these activities:

- Practising mindfulness
- Immersing yourself in nature
- Doing yoga
- Meditating
- Listening to music
  - Exercising
    - Volunteering

Happiness is a mindset for your journey, not the result of your destination.

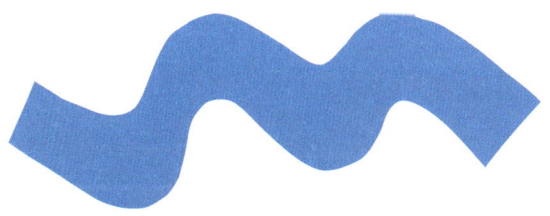

Shawn Achor

BEFRIEND YOUR BRAIN

Humans spend a lot of time in their own heads, so it makes sense to befriend our brains and embrace everything they can tell us about ourselves – especially if it's going to help us spark joy and find happiness.

Welcome the moments you spend on your own, when you're not worrying about other people and what they're thinking. You can explore your feelings, ideas, thoughts, values and goals away from any outside influence. It can also help you work through problems and find solutions. Most importantly, though, you'll be spending time with someone incredible – you.

MAKE GRATITUDE YOUR GOAL

We're all guilty of wanting to populate our lives with "things". The latest fashion brands, a fancy car, a new smartphone – whether it's something big with a high price tag or something small that we just *have* to have, it's easy to trick our brains into thinking that having more of the same will make our lives better and happier. But if we can learn to appreciate all that we're already fortunate to have, rather than spending our time and energy going after what we don't have, we'll experience more joy and less disappointment.

Next time you're feeling frustrated, take a moment to appreciate the mundane. Maybe it's seeing the birds in the trees or the smell of some freshly cut summer grass – or even just acknowledging that you have air in your lungs and a roof over your head. Finding something to be grateful for every day reminds us that joy can be found all around us – we just need to remember to look for it in the right places.

Merriment comes in sparks, joy in flashes, and happiness in lightnings.

Henry Stanley Haskins

There are so many great things in life; why dwell on negativity?

Zendaya

FEEL YOUR EMOTIONS

Sometimes we think it's easier to pack our emotions away in a box, especially negative ones. But if we keep our emotions hidden, they tend to eat away at us from the inside. And while they're doing that, they're also stifling our sense of joy. Instead, acknowledge all your feelings, both good and bad. Let them have their moment to wash over you. If you need to spend time crying, then do it. If you need to share how you're feeling with a loved one, do that, too. The important thing is to give the feeling airtime then move forwards with a more joyful outlook.

*Feelings are much like waves;
we can't stop them from coming,
but we can choose which one to surf.*

Jonatan Mårtensson

SHARE THE JOY

If you're letting all your negative emotions out of the box, then it's doubly important to let the happy ones out, too. If your day is shaping up to be an awesome one, take a moment to sit with how it's making you feel – and then share how happy you're feeling with someone else. If you're giving off a joyful vibe, it'll be almost impossible for others not to soak it up and start sparking joy in their own days, too.

DEALING WITH ANXIETY

First things first: anxiety is a completely normal response to a stressful situation. While it may cause discomfort, such as a racing heart or sweaty palms, it's actually the brain's way of protecting us. When we face a perceived threat (such as a giant bear or, more likely, a job interview), the brain sends signals to mobilize the body for action. However, frequent episodes of anxiety can become a real issue. They can drain your joy and it can be difficult to experience happiness when anxious thoughts take over. Constant anxiety can even overshadow positive emotions, leaving you stuck in a cycle of worry.

While we can't eliminate anxiety entirely – after all, it can be a motivator in some situations – we don't want it dominating our lives. The key to dealing with it is acknowledging its presence and learning how to manage it. It's like reluctantly greeting an old, annoying friend who won't leave but understanding that this "friend" doesn't have to take over your life. Over the following pages, we'll explore strategies to manage anxiety, focusing on how you can spend as little time with it as possible and embrace a sense of calmness instead.

TAKE A MINDFULNESS MINIBREAK

Mindfulness practices, such as deep breathing and meditation, are excellent tools for calming an anxious mind. They have something in common, too – the ability to ground you in the present moment and reduce worry about the future. The good news is that the only equipment you'll need is an open mind. Here's a simple exercise to give your brain a mindfulness minibreak:

1. Find a quiet space, then close your eyes and take deep, slow breaths.
2. Focus on the sensation of your breath entering and leaving your body.
3. If your mind wanders, gently return your attention to your breath.

The only limit to our realization of tomorrow will be our doubts of today.

Franklin D. Roosevelt

TAKE A MEDITATIVE MOMENT

Meditation is the ultimate example of your brain and body working harmoniously together. It can ease anxiety, boost your mood and even help you sleep better. Here's how to do it:

1. Set aside 10 to 15 minutes, sitting somewhere comfortably.
2. Close your eyes and focus on your senses. Notice what you can feel, hear, smell, touch and even taste.
3. Next, inhale while saying "breathe in" in your head. Then exhale, saying "breathe out". Focus on this circular breath, letting go of any tension as you exhale.
4. Finally, imagine warm light.

Your mind will believe everything you tell it, so make sure you feed it joy, hope and love

FIND YOUR HAPPY PLACE

Cultivating a happy mind means being brave enough to take a deep dive into your thoughts, values and emotions. This can sometimes be tough, but the awareness that comes from self-reflection will allow you to understand what makes you happy – and, ultimately, how doing more of those things can bring you joy. Here's how to find your happy place:

- Explore what values in life are important to you and reflect on the activities that resonate with them, whether it's pursuing creative goals, helping other people or advocating for a cause you're passionate about.
- Think of the moments when you feel most at peace. Are they when you're with certain people, partaking in a hobby or achieving a goal? Being aware of when you're at your happiest means you can identify what brings you joy.
- What lights you up and sparks excitement in your life? Whether its crafting, playing sports, wild swimming or travelling to far-flung locations, if it makes you feel fulfilled, you can't go wrong!

Do more of what makes you happy

Take time to make yourself your top priority

BANISH THE BAD STUFF

If identifying what makes us happiest is the key to a joyful life, working out what makes us feel bad – and then doing less of it – will boost our joy levels even more.

> Reflect on the past week and rate your activities: 1 = awful and 10 = awesome. Can you see any patterns emerging? If you're consistently giving something a low rating, could you do less of it?

Some things are, of course, unavoidable (think annoying relatives and dentist appointments), but if it's not compulsory and it brings you zero joy engaging with it, are you really going to miss it?

Happiness has to do with your mindset, not with outside circumstance.

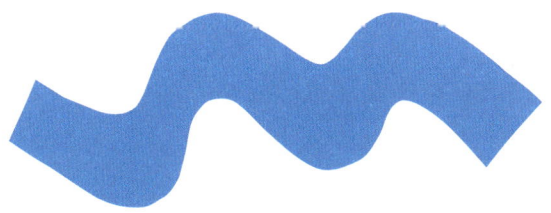

Steve Maraboli

DON'T PUT YOURSELF DOWN

Humans seem to tune in to one wavelength when they're engaging with their self-talk, and it goes a bit like this: "Everyone does life better than me", "Why am I so useless?" or "I'm so boring to be around." And so on and so on, ad infinitum.

Apart from being untrue, this negative self-talk robs you of joy. If you can learn to replace negative chatter with affirmations of compassion, capability and resilience, you can shift your mindset towards a more optimistic perspective, as well as cultivate a healthier relationship with yourself. It's a simple yet impactful way to promote lasting joy and happiness.

WAVE GOODBYE TO WORRIES

It's normal for humans to worry – after all, as a species, we're hardwired for survival, so if no one worried about anyone or anything, the world would descend into chaos. The problem is that worries can take up a lot of headspace, meaning there's no room left for joy and happiness. And many of our worries – such as fretting about how our lives compare to other people's – aren't even worth holding on to. If this sounds familiar, it's time to find a way to let the worries go.

WRITE YOUR WORRIES AWAY

Jotting down worries in a journal can help manage intrusive thoughts. It's a little like offloading to a non-judgemental friend. If your worries relate to daily tasks and accomplishing all your chores, projects or work/life admin, create a to-do list in priority order so you have a plan to follow without juggling it all in your head. Sometimes, the simple act of writing a worry down can help you see a solution – whether to show you that you need to take action to resolve it or to help you realize you're wasting mental energy on something trivial. Either way, you can let it go and, most importantly, you'll free up vital headspace for more joyful thoughts – hurrah!

If you want to fly, you have to give up what weighs you down.

Roy T. Bennett

THE POWER OF POSITIVITY

Your mind is the most powerful tool you have at your disposal, and one of the best ways you can maintain a positive mindset is to look for positivity in every situation. Joyfulness isn't something that just appears or a destination you reach one day. It's a choice and something you must actively practise – and that's easier if you have a positive outlook. Take time to reflect on the conversations you've had and actions you've taken today. Consider their impact. Have they been positive and meaningful? If not, think about how you can change them. Adjust your behaviour when needed and aim to be a positive light that shines when the world seems dark.

LET JOY BE YOUR CONSTANT

Embrace the small moments of delight in your everyday life – whether it's a smile from a stranger or that warm, fuzzy feeling you get when you hear your favourite song. Remember how that moment makes you feel and file it in your mental joy library. When joy becomes your default, it shifts your perspective, helping you start to see opportunities instead of obstacles, and gratitude instead of negativity. By making joy a constant, you not only improve your own well-being but also spark that energy in others. That's the power of sparking joy.

CHAPTER THREE

HAPPY BODY

Having a happy body is about tuning into how it feels, honouring its needs and nurturing it with joy. After all, when it comes to body positivity, it's not what your body looks like but what it can do – and the joy it allows you to experience – that matters.

By introducing small, positive habits, you can create a foundation of health and happiness. Whether it's through mindful movement and staying active, ensuring you eat a balanced diet or simply practising daily self-care, this chapter will help you nurture joy from within. Are you ready to treat your body like the ally it is? Let's get stuck in!

You are enough,
exactly as you are

Just because I don't look like everybody else doesn't mean that I can't be just as beautiful.

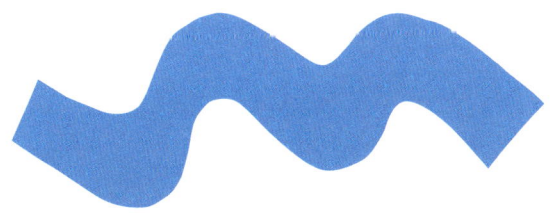

Cynthia Erivo

LEARN TO LOVE YOUR BODY

Loving your body and showing it daily gratitude for all the amazing things it does is just as important as loving your brain. In fact, if you can encourage your brain and body to get along, you'll be giving yourself the best opportunity to spark joy in all areas of your life.

Start by shifting your focus from how your body looks to how it feels. Pay attention to the sensations in your body when you move, stretch or relax. Celebrate its strength, resilience and ability to experience all life has to offer. Practise gratitude for the little things and remember that self-love comes from appreciating what your body does for you daily.

Being comfortable in your own skin, no matter your size or shape, frees up more headspace that you can invest in the things that make you happy, whether that's hiking up a mountain or cosying up with a cat and a good book. But best of all, it brings us the joy of inner peace. Remember, we only get one body, so it's time to start loving it!

PRACTISE BODY-POSITIVE AFFIRMATIONS

Affirmations are short, positive statements that lift us up when we're feeling low. They're also a brilliant tool for resetting our brains to "body-positive" mode if we've been caught in a spiral of body-bashing. The best thing is that if we say affirmations to ourselves enough, we start to believe them. Not convinced? Try repeating some of these next time you need a boost:

- "I am thankful for my body."
- "My body deserves to be loved."
- "I decide my own worth."
- "My weight doesn't define me."
- "Loving my body is a commitment to a joyful life."

You can be whatever size you are, and you can be beautiful both inside and out.

Serena Williams

Plus-size?

More like my size.

Ashley Graham

FIND YOUR BALANCE

Loving your body doesn't mean forcing yourself to celebrate or accentuate the bits you find hard to like. If loving your body is something you struggle with, for now aim for body neutrality instead. This means cultivating a more balanced view of your body and accepting it as it is. In time, you might come to love the way you look and reach a place of body-positive joy, but right now remember your worth isn't determined by your looks. Body image is just one piece of the puzzle, after all, so focus on other qualities that define you: your personality, kindness, skills, resilience and the strength you show in overcoming challenges.

Every curve, crease or mark on your body tells a story of strength and resilience

CREATE YOUR OWN DEFINITION OF BEAUTY

On social media and online, "beauty" is often defined by appearance alone. It overlooks our inner qualities and the diversity all around us. But if we accept this narrow definition, it leads to a lifetime of body dissatisfaction – and notions of beauty become a beast of society's making. By creating our own definitions of beauty, we take back control and stop worrying about other people's standards, reducing the urge to compare ourselves negatively. Think about your loved ones – friends, family and others in your life. What qualities make them truly beautiful to you? Chances are how they look doesn't even figure.

MOVE MORE JOYFULLY

Moving joyfully isn't about skipping around the supermarket or prancing into your next doctor's appointment (although by all means do those things if they bring you joy!). Instead, it's about engaging in physical activities that make your mind and body feel alive and happy. Whether it's dancing, walking in nature or playing a sport, moving joyfully helps you connect with your body and encourages you to celebrate how it feels – not how it looks or how it's performing. If movement becomes a choice, rather than a chore, you know you're onto a winner.

BETTER SLEEP = BETTER HEALTH

Sleep is vital to emotional well-being. In a 2018 study, published in *Frontiers in Psychology*, the participants who reported better sleep quality tended to state higher levels of life satisfaction and happiness. So if sleep can help us achieve a joyful life, how do we get more of it? Follow these simple steps to give you the best possible chance:

- Stick to a consistent sleep schedule – go to bed and wake up at the same time every day. Yes, even on weekends.
- Establish a relaxing routine before bed, such as reading, journalling or taking a warm bath.
- Avoid screens for at least 30 minutes before bed.
- Avoid caffeine, alcohol and large meals at least 3 to 4 hours before bed.
- Exercise regularly to enjoy deeper sleep, but not too close to bedtime or you'll be too wired to fall asleep.
- Get exposure to natural light during the day, to help regulate your circadian rhythm.
- Keep your bedroom for sleep – try not to use it for activities such as watching TV or working, so your brain associates it with sleep.

You're wonderful and awesome and perfect.

Jonah Hill

You define beauty yourself. Society doesn't define your beauty.

Lady Gaga

LIMIT YOUR SCREEN TIME

Reducing the time you spend looking at screens and scheduling offline activities instead nurtures a happy body and mind. Try setting yourself specific boundaries for when and how long you'll be on your device. Start by scheduling screen-free times that are easy to stick to, such as during meals or before bed, to help you unplug. You could even set a daily reminder to take a break. Use the time you've gained to engage in offline activities, such as exercising or spending time outdoors, and experience the joy of real-life interactions instead.

To be yourself in a world that is constantly trying to make you something else is the greatest accomplishment.

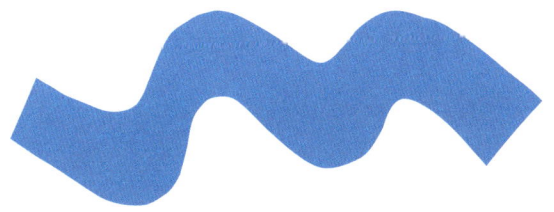

Ralph Waldo Emerson

True beauty radiates from self-acceptance and love

People often say that beauty is in the eye of the beholder, and I say that the most liberating thing about beauty is realizing that you are the beholder.

Salma Hayek

STOP SCROLLING

We're all guilty of getting sucked into the social media scroll. We might feel like we're in control, but those algorithms just keep getting cleverer, which makes it harder for us to filter unhelpful content from our feeds. But we can nurture a healthy body image *and* enjoy social media by following these tips:

- Curate your feed to include positive, authentic and diverse accounts that promote body positivity.
- Unfollow content that makes you feel inadequate or that sees you comparing yourself to others.
- Set daily time limits on social media apps, to prevent mindless scrolling.

Remind yourself that social media doesn't reflect reality.

Taking care of our bodies physically also nurtures our minds, making it one of the best forms of self-care. Exercise releases endorphins (the feel-good hormones), which boost our mood and help us feel more positive, reducing anxiety and increasing energy and confidence.

We all know the science behind it – but how do we make it happen? If regular exercise is already a favourite part of your routine, that's brilliant! But if reading this makes you want to cry, that's OK, too. If working out feels more like a chore than a joy, focus on activities that excite you, not ones you feel you "should" do. Try casting your mind back to the activities you enjoyed as a child. Perhaps it was one of these:

- Skateboarding
- Hula-hooping
- Mountain biking
- Roller-skating
- Skipping
- Karate
- Gymnastics
- Table tennis

Could one of these fun-filled activities become a new fitness hobby for you?

LOOK AFTER THE SKIN YOU'RE IN

Your skin is the largest organ you have, so it's important to look after it – after all, it protects everything that happens inside you, as well as helping you sense and feel your environment so you can live joyfully. Having a healthy glow might also boost your confidence, and the act of practising a skincare routine can be a calming ritual, giving you a moment of self-care in your day to help reduce stress. Adopt a routine that includes cleansing, moisturizing and sun protection so you have a barrier against environmental damage. It's time to love the skin you're in!

CREATE A JOYFUL WARDROBE

If your wardrobe looks a little "safe" these days and you're finding you're stuck in an outfit rut, mixing things up and experimenting with some new looks can help lift your mood and spark joy. There's an unwritten rule of adulting that says we can't dress too outlandishly for fear of judgement – but this is nonsense and, in any case, rules are there to be broken. Have fun with your wardrobe. Be wild, be wacky – but most importantly, wear whatever puts a smile on your face and makes you happy.

If you retain nothing else, always remember the most important rule of beauty, which is: who cares?

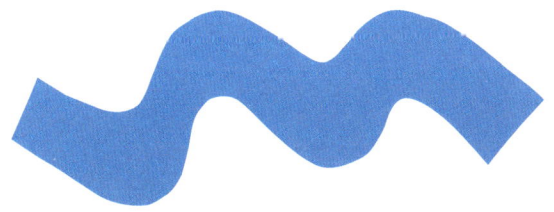

Tina Fey

FIND JOY IN EATING WELL

Eating foods that make our bodies healthy and happy doesn't always mean sticking to the "right" foods or counting calories. It's all about balance. We know the importance of nutrition for maintaining a healthy body, but if the sight of yet another berry smoothie or tub of hummus makes you want to scream, it might be time to temporarily cut yourself a bit of slack and indulge in a treat (or two).

HAPPY SNACKING

A study published in the *Journal of Nutritional Biochemistry* found that consuming 30 g (1 oz) of 85 per cent cocoa dark chocolate can boost our emotional well-being. Treating ourselves to something tasty every so often also enhances the release of dopamine, a feel-good neurotransmitter, which helps improve mood and reduce stress.

Most importantly, have fun with food and don't sweat over a slice of cake. A balanced approach contributes to a healthier relationship with food, fostering a positive mindset around eating. And if we love what we're eating and enjoy fuelling our bodies, we'll be experiencing joy every time we tuck in.

Nourish your body and nurture your mind

A healthy body empowers you to live joyfully

STRETCH REGULARLY

There's a lot to be said for a really good stretch, especially those first-thing-in-the-morning stretches, when we feel compelled to let out a big sigh at the end. Incorporating a stretching routine into your day offers numerous benefits for both your body and mind. It helps improve flexibility, which you'll need for all that joyful movement, and will help prevent injury and maintain flexibility as you age. It also reduces muscle tension and alleviates stress – both of which lend themselves to a more joyful state of being. It may be a simple act, but it's an effective way to nurture your well-being.

Take care of your body. It's the only place you have to live.

Jim Rohn

REST AND RECOVERY

It's not just physical exercise that puts a strain on your body. Stress, inadequate sleep, illness and injury can also affect how much get-up-and-go you have – and can mean you're less likely to be in the right frame of mind for sparking joy. Sometimes it's OK to prioritize rest rather than trying to push through. Resting allows your body to repair muscles, reduces fatigue and replenishes energy stores. You can still engage in light activities, such as stretching, but try to focus on hydration, nutrition and – most importantly – resting so you feel fully recovered and ready for another day.

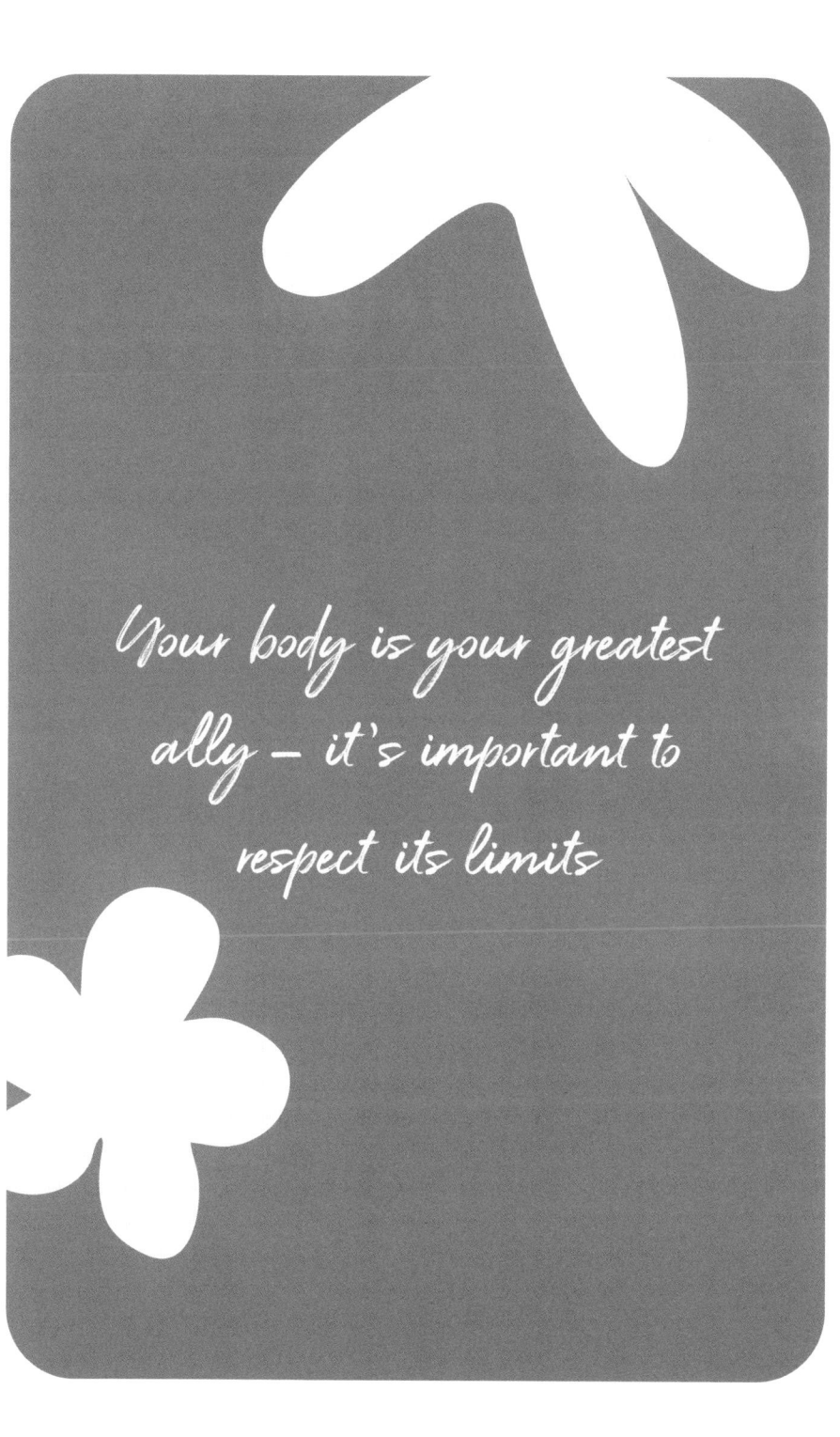

PAY ATTENTION TO YOUR BODY'S CUES

When we're busy, it's easy to forget even the basic needs of our bodies. Hands up if you've ever been so caught up in something that you've forgotten to eat, drink or take a comfort break. The problem is, when we ignore our bodies' signals and push aside cues such as thirst, hunger and fatigue, we aren't showing ourselves the compassion we deserve or encouraging a body-positive mindset. Most of the time, our bodies have our backs, so it's about time we repaid them by actually *listening* to them. Try following these tips:

- Don't ignore your body's signals. Make a conscious effort to notice feelings of hunger, tiredness or discomfort, and ask yourself what your body needs in order to feel better.
- Be aware of your inner critic, especially when it contradicts your body's needs. For example, "Finish the dishes before lunch" or "Don't eat until you've worked out." Don't let these thoughts override what your body is telling you.
- Show respect to your body by acting on its requests and it will repay you by giving you the energy to spark joy each and every day!

CHAPTER FOUR

JOYFUL LIFE

Life is filled with distractions and challenges, and living joyfully can often feel elusive. Sometimes it can even feel like everyone else is managing it, except you – you're just hanging in there. But living a joyful life is not about luck or even circumstance. Instead, it's a conscious choice rooted in your mindset and actions.

In this final chapter, we'll explore how to cultivate and maintain joy – a process that starts from within. By nurturing self-awareness, gratitude and meaningful connections, anyone can create a life filled with happiness. It all starts with a simple intention: to choose joy.

Let joy ignite
your journey!

HAPPY HOBBY, HAPPY LIFE

Having a hobby you love means you can tap into an unlimited supply of joyfulness whenever you partake in it. If you can carve out a little corner of every day to do whatever it is that makes your heart feel happy, it's the ultimate act of self-care.

Maybe you're keen to try something new and different, or perhaps you've let an old hobby lapse, forgetting how good it used to make you feel. Whatever your chosen activity, the sky's the limit! As long as it makes you feel alive and you look forward to the next time you'll get to do it, you're on to a winner.

To give your hobby the best chance of making a meaningful impact on your happiness levels, it's important to make time for it – which is often easier said than done when you have a hundred and one things on your to-do list. Try scheduling a dedicated hobby morning or afternoon into your week and make it sacred so no one can interfere with your plans!

LET GO OF REGRETS

No one wants to look back on their life with regret. While we may stumble on our journeys through life, the goal is to grow old reflecting on a life full of joy. To help you let go of your regrets, consider the philosophies you want to live by. Core values, such as living authentically, maintaining balance and respecting personal boundaries, can guide you. Start today: which philosophies could help you live with fewer regrets? What values will shape your choices?

STEP OUT OF YOUR COMFORT ZONE

Familiarity can be comforting, but sometimes we can get too comfortable in our safe zones, leaving ourselves with less opportunity to experience the joy of doing something different. By stepping out of our comfort zones, we can open the door to new experiences and enrich our lives. By embracing change, you'll be fostering a growth mindset, which will ultimately help you navigate life's uncertainties with confidence and optimism, and spark joy in the most challenging of circumstances. Is there something new you could challenge yourself to experience?

LOVE TO LAUGH

Laughing isn't just good for the soul – it's essential for our physical well-being. It reduces stress, lowers pain levels and enhances overall happiness by triggering the release of endorphins. But most importantly, laughter also strengthens our connections with others, making interactions more joyful and creating a sense of shared experience. Best of all, it's free – and contagious! Here are some ideas to get you started:

- Throw a games party. Silly games such as Twister and charades are classic crowd-pleasers that are guaranteed to get everyone giggling.
- Have a romcom marathon with popcorn and your favourite people, and share the joy of laughing together.
- Go to a live comedy club – the contagious effect of laughter means you'll giggle even more.
- If something silly or ridiculous happened to you today, share it with a loved one – you'll be able to relive the humour of the situation and make someone else laugh, too.

You'll probably find you experience more moments of laughter when you live life joyfully. Being light-hearted and finding something to laugh about, even in moments of frustration, gives you – and those around you – even more to giggle at.

I honestly think it's the thing I like most, to laugh.

Audrey Hepburn

Joy is not in things;

it is in us.

Richard Wagner

EXPERIENCE THE GREAT OUTDOORS

There's something uniquely joyful about taking a big breath of fresh coastal air or kicking up the autumn leaves. As well as sparking joy, spending time in nature offers numerous well-being benefits. A 2019 study published in *Frontiers in Psychology* compared the effects of nature on cognitive performance with those of urban settings and showed that natural environments enhance mood, reduce stress, boost cognitive performance and reduce mental fatigue. Exercising in nature is also a great way to boost cardiovascular health and enjoy scenic views at the same time. Most importantly, being outdoors fosters joy, creativity, mindfulness and a deeper connection to the environment, enhancing overall happiness. It's not called the great outdoors for nothing!

The more you praise and celebrate your life, the more there is in life to celebrate.

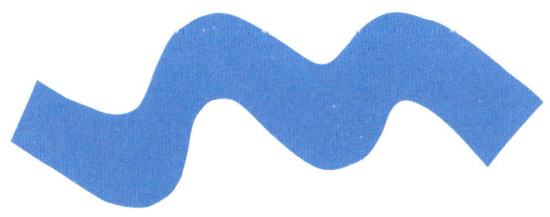

Oprah Winfrey

CELEBRATE YOUR WINS

Knowing you've achieved something – no matter how small – is guaranteed to boost your joy levels. But many of us have an annoying habit of downplaying our successes. It's as though being proud of ourselves somehow makes us seem a bit smug, or worse, arrogant. But if you have something to be proud of, revel in your achievement and stop undermining your hard work. Start giving yourself credit instead. Whatever it is you've done well, no matter how (un)impressive you think it is to others, celebrate your win and tell anyone who'll listen. You've earned those bragging rights!

NURTURE YOUR FRIENDSHIPS

You know when you've hit the friendship jackpot when your relationship just feels "right". It's a judgement-free zone, so you can be utterly honest with the other person without them flouncing from the room in a strop. You can agree to disagree and move on without a second thought. They're your biggest cheerleader and don't bat an eyelid when you do something ridiculous. You've seen them at their lowest and they've seen you looking even worse. And so on.

Once-in-a-lifetime forever friendships like this are the very essence of a joyful experience, and the science is there to back this up. In an 80-year study into happiness by Harvard Medical School, data proved that the quality of our relationships is the key indicator of joy and happiness. It also found that the participants who were most satisfied in their friendships at the age of 50 were the healthiest and happiest at age 80. So it's official: nurturing our closest friendships is one of the simplest ways to spark joy, allowing us to live a life that's as happy as it can possibly be. And all that joyfulness will help us live longer, too. Hurray!

SPEND TIME SOCIALIZING

Now we know how important friendships are, what's the best way to keep sparking that joy? While a quick check-in via text is a handy way to connect, it's less meaningful than spending time with your favourite people in real life, so focus on quality over quantity. Show a genuine interest in each other's lives and plan activities that everyone enjoys, whether it's a simple walk or trying something new together. Be present, let go of distractions (put that phone down!) and embrace spontaneity. Celebrate each other's successes and support each other through challenges – all this combined will help maintain your precious bond of shared joy and connection.

A true friend is the one who holds your hand and touches your heart.

Gabriel García Márquez

HOW TO HANDLE CHANGING RELATIONSHIPS

Being human is all about connection – it's our ability to form emotional and intellectual bonds that has enabled humanity to survive and thrive.

Our relationships influence not only our well-being but also our ability to innovate, solve problems and adapt to challenges – all of which help bring joy into our own lives and the lives of those around us. But sometimes a relationship can have the opposite effect – and maintaining that connection can become a burden. If you have a relationship in your life that's no longer serving you, consider the following:

- If you want to maintain the relationship, start by fostering healthy communication. Be honest about how their behaviour impacts you (or potentially vice versa) and set clear boundaries.
- Boundaries evolve over time, so maintain open conversations, especially if the relationship is strained and you're working to rebuild it.
- Allow space and time for change. Healing takes time, so give each other room to grow.
- If things aren't improving or your boundaries aren't being respected, letting the relationship go completely might be better for everyone. Though difficult, remember that prioritizing your well-being will lead to brighter, more joyful days ahead.

LEARNING FOR LIFE

When was the last time you learned a new skill? A study published in *Arts & Health* found that one of the ways we can live a joyful life is to learn something new and challenge ourselves. Not only does learning create new brain connections, but it also helps us feel empowered. It also broadens our perspectives – of others, of the world, of circumstances and of possibilities – all of which correlate with greater happiness and lasting joy. Best of all, mastering a new skill is something to feel proud of. Start with small, achievable steps, such as learning to cook a new recipe. Enjoy the process and let curiosity lead the way!

Small, intentional actions can create a lasting sense of well-being and joy

Embrace what brings you joy; let go of what holds you back

Joy is a state of being we can nurture every day

A SPARK IN THE DARK

Joy is often the hardest emotion to muster when we're having an off day. But we all have that one thing that gives us a boost when we need it most. These things will all have something in common: they bring us that feel-good, joy-sparking energy when we're feeling low. What's yours? Anything that recharges your positivity levels counts, whether it's playing loud music (air guitar optional), hanging out with a friend who always lifts you up or taking a peaceful moment to reflect. Don't fumble about in the dark – use a spark to light things up.

*Be happy with being you.
Love your flaws. Own your quirks.*

Ariana Grande

SET A JOYFUL INTENTION

If you ever feel like joy is passing you by, you can take back control by setting a joyful intention. Unlike goal setting, intentions focus on the behaviour or practice we want to manifest, rather than a specific outcome. Whether we set them daily or weekly, they can help us live with purpose and authenticity, as well as ensuring our actions align with our life values. For example, "Today my intention is to finish my project with joy and determination." It's a really useful tool for helping us stay focused on joy, even when times are challenging.

MAKE YOUR GOALS JOYFUL

Goal setting can seem a little daunting. After all, goals come with a set of expectations and responsibilities and the possibility of failure. But research suggests people who have goals they're working towards are happier than those without them. Goals provide structure and meaning, as well as boosting our self-esteem. And, ultimately, they can help us maximize the joy in our lives. Here's how to do it:

- Start by identifying what excites you – whether it's a passion, relationship or personal development goal. Make sure you align your goals with what brings you the most happiness and fulfilment.
- Break your goals down into achievable steps that allow for progress while maintaining joy in the journey.
- Ensure your goals reflect your values and purpose so you're inspired to achieve them. Celebrate every milestone and enjoy the journey, rather than just focusing on the destination.

When you create goals that nurture your happiness, you're more likely to stay motivated, maintain a positive mindset and embrace each step with enthusiasm, making the pursuit just as rewarding as the achievement.

They say a person needs just three things to be truly happy in this world: someone to love, something to do and something to hope for.

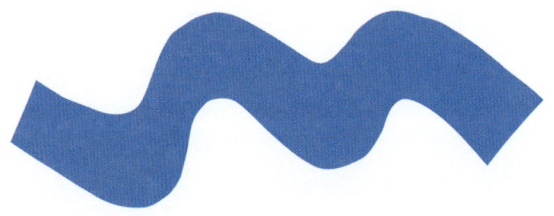

Tom Bodett

KNOW YOUR "WHY"

Inside each of us is a purpose. It's like a driving force that propels us on a meaningful journey through life. It's personally significant and has the potential to make a positive impact on the world. It's the reason we keep going when things get tough, and it often sustains us when we're feeling a little lost and need a helping hand back to the right path. Living with purpose goes hand in hand with living a joyful life – so tap into your passions and pursue what excites you. In doing so, you'll be hitting the joy jackpot!

Joy is the best makeup.
If you're happy, it shows.

Anne Lamott

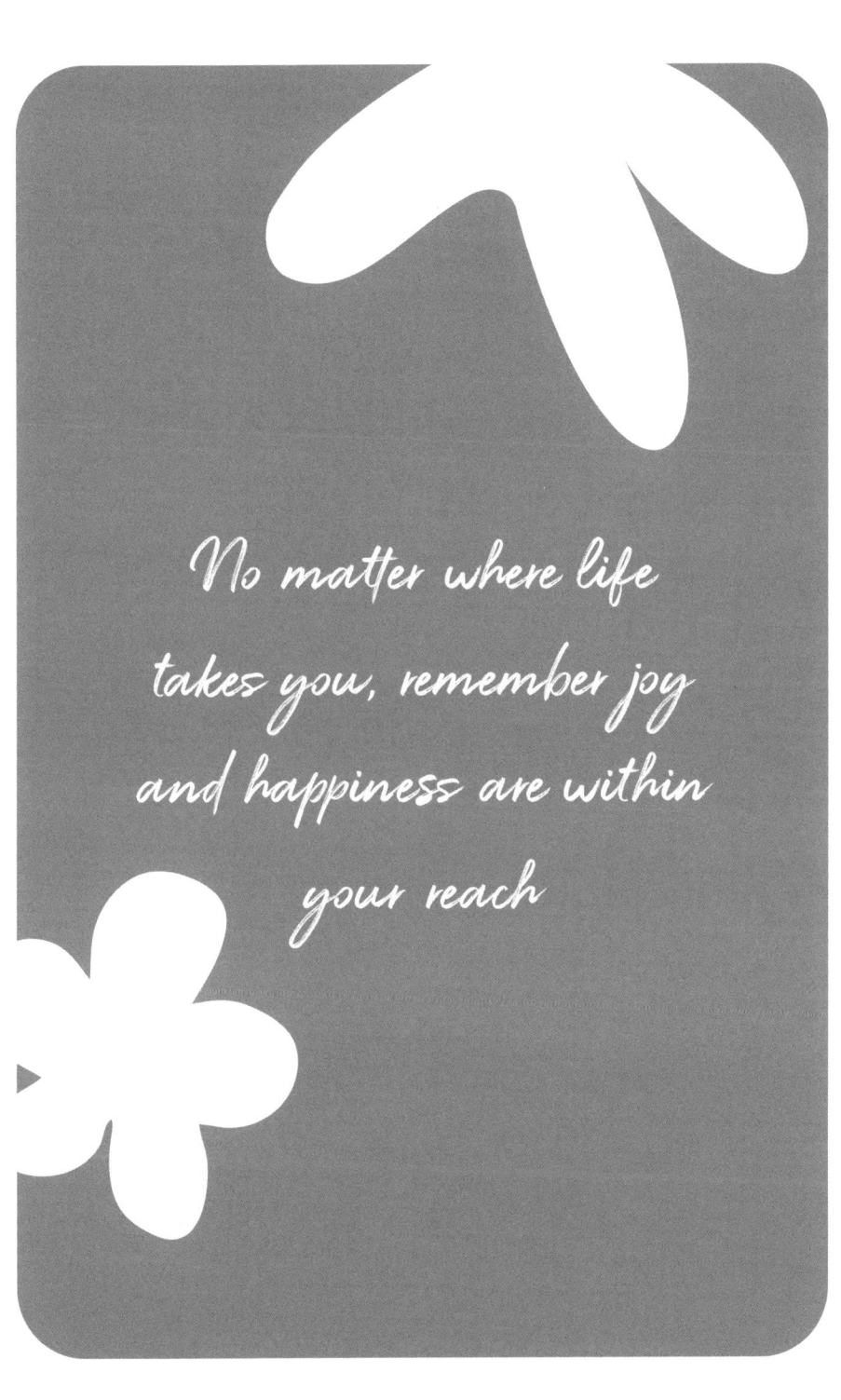

CONCLUSION

Now you've finished this book, remember that joy is not a destination but a way of living. We can find it every day – in moments of stillness and reflection, in the laughter shared with loved ones, and in the simple act of embracing each new day.

If you ever need a little lift, these pages will be here for you as a constant companion on your joyful journey, lighting the way even on the toughest of days. Each and every one of us is deserving of a life filled with joy, so aim to carry its spark within you and allow it not only to encourage joy in others but also to guide you through life's difficulties – because that's when the impact of living joyfully is felt the most. Always remember that joy is yours to create, no matter where you are or what you face. You've got this!

How to Ease Your Anxiety

Embrace Calm and Say Goodbye to Worries for Good

Sophie Golding
Paperback
ISBN: 978-1-83799-379-6

Calm your mind

Life is full of beautiful, joyous experiences just waiting to be had. But when you struggle with anxiety, your brain can come up with all sorts of reasons not to do the things you love. By learning to ease anxious thinking and restore a sense of calm, you can start to live the life of your dreams in peace and serenity.

Through simple tips and kind advice, this book will show you how to tune out negative thinking and find mental tranquillity.

How to Romanticize Your Life

Joyful Tips and Advice to Elevate Every Day

Sophie Golding
Hardback
ISBN: 978-1-83799-466-3

Make everyday moments dazzle

Sometimes the best things in life are the simplest: a good book, the soft pitter-patter of rain, the feel of grass beneath bare feet. If we could fill our lives with these small pleasures, just think how lovely our world could be.

Learn how to elevate every day with this stunning guide to finding joy in everything you do. With the help of the tips and advice inside, you'll soon be on the path to a life that's filled with gratitude, self-kindness and simple, magical moments.

Have you enjoyed this book?

If so, why not write a review on your favourite website?

If you're interested in finding out more about our books, find us on Facebook at **Summersdale Publishers**, on Twitter/X at **@Summersdale** and on Instagram, TikTok and Bluesky at **@summersdalebooks** and get in touch. We'd love to hear from you!

Thanks very much for buying this Summersdale book.

www.summersdale.com

Image Credits

All images © GoodStudio/Shutterstock.com